"Journey of a Grieving Heart"

30 DEVOTIONS AND TIPS FOR FINDING PEACE AND EMBRACING LIFE AFTER THE LOSS OF A LOVED ONE

Shannon Joy Johnson

Copyright © 2024 Shannon J. Johnson

ALL RIGHTS RESERVED.

Scripture references are taken from the
New Living Translation (NLT),
the New International Version (NIV), or
the King James Version (KJV) of the Bible.

DISCLAIMERS

This body of literature is intended for informational and inspirational purposes only. While the information provided are based on the author's personal experiences and reflections, they are not a substitute for professional, medical, psychological, or therapeutic advice.

The author is not a licensed therapist, counselor, or medical professional. Readers are encouraged to seek professional help if they are struggling with their grief or if they require specific medical or psychological support.

This body of literature is designed to offer guidance and support as you navigate the grieving process, but individual results may vary. The effectiveness of the information described cannot be guaranteed.

The views expressed in this body of literature are those of the author alone and do not necessarily reflect the opinions or beliefs of any affiliates, organizations, or institutions.

By reading this body of literature, you acknowledge that the author and publisher are not liable for any actions taken based on the content provided.

TABLE OF CONTENTS

WELCOME

Explore how my personal journey through grief inspired the creation of this body of literature.

JOURNEY OF A GRIEVING HEART: DEVOTIONS & TIPS

Consists of thirty helpful and practical tips to guide you through your journey, including worksheets, affirmations, self-care activities, and bible scriptures.

CONCLUSION

A final reflection of finding hope and healing after loss, summarizing key sights and offering encouragement for continuing the journey forward.

"JOURNEY OF A GRIEVING HEART"

WELCOME

On August 23, 2022, my world changed forever. That day, my Mommy—my best friend, my workout partner, my #1 cheerleader—suddenly passed away. The loss of my mother shattered everything I knew, leaving me heartbroken and adrift.

What followed was a journey of grief and growth, as I learned to adjust to a new reality—living without the woman who had been my everything. For over thirty years, our home had been made up of my mom, my dad, and myself. But suddenly, it was just my dad and I, and I had to find a way to move forward in a world without her.

As I walked this painful path, I began to discover small, yet powerful tips that helped me navigate the raw emotions and find moments of peace amid the sorrow. These insights were helpful to me during the toughest days, and I believe they can offer healing to others who are also trying to embrace life after the loss of a loved one.

It is with great love and hope that I present this book, "Journey of a Grieving Heart: 30 Devotions and Tips for Finding Peace and Embracing Life After the Loss of a Loved One." May these devotions and tips help you, along your own journey.

With Love,

Shannon Joy

LET HIM IN.

1

Invite God into your journey to healing. Believe it or not, He's the one who is going to give you joy in times of weakness; He's going to give you peace that surpasses all understanding; He's going to make a way out of no way; He's going to mend your broken heart; He's the one that will never leave you nor forsake you and be right by your side to wipe your tears, especially when the phone calls and visits become less and less.

2

FORGIVE.

Forgive God, Forgive Your Loved One that passed away, Forgive those that hurt you, and Forgive Yourself. You may be mad at God for taking your loved one away; you maybe mad at your loved one for leaving you here on Earth; you may be mad at those who hurt you by not showing up for you when you needed them the most; you may be mad at yourself, wondering about the wouldas, couldas, and shouldas. Forgive anyway. Unforgiveness can become a distraction that can delay your healing and block the blessings in store for you.

JOURNEY OF A GRIEVING HEART

EMBRACING MY GRIEF

1.) How are you feeling today?

2.) What is one thing you miss the most about the person you lost?

3.) What things have been different since the loss?

4.) Who are the people supporting you?

5.) How do you take care of yourself as you experience grief?

Trust in the Lord with all of your heart and lean not to your own understanding.

Proverbs 3:5-6 (KJV)

YOUR *Notes*:

CHECK ON YOUR BILLS.

3

When you're grieving, the last thing on your mind is Bills; however, if you don't check on your Bills, it will suffer. Before you know it, your credit score would have tremendously decreased by not staying on top of it. Make it a habit to go over your Bills. You may have to do this a few times a month. You may have to adjust your Bills to accommodate new expenses due to your loved ones's passing. Place your Bills on Auto-Pay if you need to. Don't be afraid to reach out to the Billing Company to change the bill's due date or even set-up a payment plan. You'd be surprised, some companies are understanding and willing to assist you any way that they possibly can. If you're having trouble with the Bills, communicate with the Billing Company sooner rather than later. The last thing you want, especially while grieving, is to jeopardize your livelihood.

PRACTICE SELF-CARE.

4

The overwhelmness of your loved one's passing can take a toll on you, but practicing self-care can help you combat those overwhelming and anxious feelings. It is extremely important to make sure that you are balanced mentally, physically, emotionally, and spiritually. Incorporate self-care days regularly. Do something for yourself no matter how big or small. This can be something as simple as reading a book, going to the gym, going to the spa, drinking a warm glass of tea, or going on a vacation, just to name few.

JOURNEY OF A GRIEVING HEART

Daily Affirmations

Today, I open my heart to divine guidance and embrace the healing power of forgiveness. I trust that letting Him into my journey and releasing past hurts will bring me peace and clarity. I will also take practical steps by managing my responsibilities with grace, checking on bills, and prioritizing self-care.

Cast your *cares*
onto
the Lord....

Psalm 55:22 (KJV)

YOUR *Notes*:

5 ALLOW THOSE WHO LOVE YOU TO LOVE ON YOU.

These are a special group of people, even if it's just one person. These people don't have to be there for you, but they made a choice to be by your side. Don't push them away. Don't lash out at them because they are there. Appreciate them; cherish them. Love them and allow them to love you. Embrace that good, positive energy.

---

6 JOURNAL.

Your Journal will become one of your best friends. The great thing about journaling is that you don't have to be the perfect writer to journal. Journaling will help you navigate through your thoughts. It will help you express your feelings, whether you're happy, sad, mad, etc. On those days when you may not have anyone to talk to, you'll always have your Journal. Keep a Journal with you, whether it's in your bedroom, your purse, your car, or use your NotePad on your phone. Sometimes you may have a thought that you need to get out right away for example, a memory of your loved one or an ingredient(s) to their special dish.

JOURNEY OF A GRIEVING HEART

Self Care ACTIVITIES

Choose any Self-Care Activity from the list below to complete today.

1. Start a journal ☐

2. Go for a 30 minute walk ☐

3. Read a book for 30 minutes ☐

4. Declutter bedroom ☐

5. Listen to calming music ☐

6. Spend the day social media free ☐

What the enemy meant for evil, God meant it for my *good.*

Genesis 50:20 (KJV)

YOUR *Notes*:

CREATE A ROUTNINE.

7

When you are grieving, you barely want to do anything. If you could lay in the bed all day and sleep the hurt away, you would, but from experience, this is not healthy and is no way to live. Creating a routine will help you get back in the swing of things. It can be that reason why you get out of the bed. It can be the reason why you step outside to get some sunlight. At first, you may have to start out with a simple routine such as getting out of the bed, making your bed, washing your face, brushing your teeth, combing your hair, taking a shower, taking your vitamins, etc. But remember no routine is too small, whatever step you're able to do is an achievement because sometimes it can take days, weeks, and months before you feel like doing anything.

8

BE THANKFUL.

Being thankful helps to change your perspective and helps you to look at the brighter side of things. It helps renew your mind and delete that stinking thinking and negative thoughts. When you feel yourself traveling down memory lane and pondering on your loved one's passing, being thankful can snap you out of it. Start out by finding one thing to be thankful for. Before you know it, you'll be able to write a whole list of things to be thankful for. Remember, no matter how bad we might think our situation is, there is someone who wishes that they were in your shoes.

JOURNEY OF A GRIEVING HEART

THE PIECES OF MY HEART

Take a moment to think about the people, things, and activities that bring joy to your heart. Use the space below to draw or write about them.

For the *joy* of the Lord is my strength.

Nehemiah 8:10 (KJV)

YOUR *Notes*:

GIVE BACK.

You might be thinking, how can I help someone else when I can barely help myself, especially at a time like this???? Well…. I'm pretty sure you've heard the saying, "it's better to give than to receive,"right? This is a true statement. Giving back can help give you a sense of purpose. Helping others is a joyful feeling. Once you begin giving back and helping others, you'll want to do it again and again.

9

CELEBRATE.

Any moment can be a reason to celebrate. Life is not guaranteed. If you were able to open your eyes; if you still have life in your body, then, CELEBRATE!!! No moment is too big or too small. If you were able to get out the bed today, I applaud you 👏 if you noticed that you cried less today, I applaud you 👏 if you were able to get dressed and hang out with your friend, I applaud you 👏 Give yourself an applause 👏

10

JOURNEY OF A GRIEVING HEART

Page 22

Daily Affirmations

Today, I embrace the love and support offered by those around me and open my heart to receive their kindness. I will journal my thoughts and feelings, creating a routine that brings me comfort and stability. I choose to be thankful for the small and large blessings in my life, giving back to others as a way of spreading positivity. I celebrate every step forward, honoring both the big and small victories on my journey.

God *blesses* those who mourn, for they will be comforted.

Matthew 5:4 (NLT)

YOUR *Notes*:

BE AWARE OF YOUR FEELINGS.

11

Be aware that your emotions can constantly be up and down, and it can come out of nowhere. For example, you may have noticed on a particular day that you are feeling kind of down but don't know why? You happen to look at the Calendar on your phone, and noticed that your loved one's birthday is soon approaching or the holidays are right around the corner; or you happen to turn on the radio and your loved one's favorite song is playing; or you turned on the TV and a show that the both of you enjoyed watching together is on the screen.

12

SET BOUNDARIES.

Setting boundaries is important during your journey to healing. Setting boundaries can have a positive effect on your mental health. Start by saying "No." If you don't want to attend an event, say No. If you're unable to commit to an assignment, say No. If you need more time to make a decision, express that. Don't say Yes if you're unsure because if you do, at the end you'll end up causing unnecessary stress to yourself. You're going through enough stress as is; therefore, keep unnecessary stress to a minimum as much as possible.

JOURNEY OF A GRIEVING HEART

Self Care ACTIVITIES

Choose any Self-Care Activity from the list below to complete today.

1. Wake up 30 minutes early ☐
2. Call someone you love ☐
3. Declutter bathroom ☐
4. Take a long shower or bath ☐
5. Create a morning routine ☐
6. Create a Gratitude List ☐

Yet what we suffer now is nothing compared to the *glory* he will reveal to us later.

Romans 8:18 (NLT)

YOUR *Notes*:

BE AWARE OF UNEXPECTED TRIGGERS.

13

Please be aware that triggers can be overwhelming, especially, when it comes out of nowhere; because you weren't expecting it, you weren't prepared on how to handle it. From my experience, the triggers that come from out of nowhere are the worst, but once I experienced it and realized what was happening, I was able to calm myself down and mentally talk myself through it. For example, when I saw the movie, " The Woman King," I noticed tears coming down my face uncontrollably. I wasn't sad, but certain parts of the movie reminded me of my Mom and I. Another example, was when I attended a family function and certain songs would play; it reminded me of how my Mom and dance partners would dance to those songs.

If you experience a trigger, I would recommend acknowledging what is happening, but don't allow it to overtake you. This is when your support system will be needed, if you need someone to talk to, talk to them or write your feelings down in your journal.

THE FIRSTS.

14

"The Firsts" of the firsts can be the worst. This is because it's "the first" occasion without your loved one. Emotions can be triggered, especially around the holidays or special occasions such as birthdays and anniversarys. For me, I try to mentally prepare myself for these occasions days in advance. Focus more on the positive memories, if possible. If your loved one was still here, what would you be doing together? Would it be going to the spa, going to a restaurant, etc.? Try celebrating the occasion the way you would if your loved one was here.

JOURNEY OF A GRIEVING HEART

EMOTIONS WORD SEARCH

Can you find the words hidden in the puzzle?

V	A	S	A	D	M	T	I	R	E	D	C
H	X	L	P	N	I	R	O	M	I	N	L
S	A	N	G	R	G	I	E	B	S	S	A
H	A	P	N	E	N	R	H	H	U	L	N
N	M	E	P	G	F	C	Y	R	R	T	E
S	S	J	O	Y	F	U	L	L	P	O	R
C	T	C	G	U	G	P	I	L	R	R	V
A	A	H	B	O	R	E	D	E	I	T	O
R	R	L	F	O	S	E	D	U	S	E	U
E	A	R	M	L	E	R	O	T	E	I	S
D	F	C	O	N	F	U	S	E	D	E	N
G	W	O	R	R	I	E	D	O	K	E	T

BORED **JOYFUL** **CONFUSED** **SAD**

ANGRY **SCARED** **SURPRISED** **CALM**

HAPPY **WORRIED** **NERVOUS** **TIRED**

God is *close* to the brokenhearted; he rescues those whose spirits are crushed.

Psalms 34:18 (NLT)

YOUR *Notes*:

MOVE YOUR BODY.

Move your body. Get up out of the bed, freshen up, and go for a walk. Get some fresh air; feel the sun's rays on your skin; listen to the birds chirping; look at the beautiful sky and trees; go for a joy ride and listen to some soothing music. Circulate the blood in your body. Once you begin moving your body, you'll want to continue and keep it up. Eventually, you'll feel motivated to start moving in other areas of your life.

15

16

EXECUTE YOUR GOALS.

As previously mentioned, once you begin moving your body and exercising, you'll be motivated to move in other areas of your life, particularly, executing your goals. I'm pretty sure before your loved one passed away, you had a of list of goals that you wanted to accomplish; you may have even shared those goals with your loved one. Now is the perfect time to execute those goals. It'll help your mind focus on something positive, get you out of that funk, and get living again.

Daily Affirmations

Today, I am mindful of my feelings and set healthy boundaries to protect my well-being. I stay aware of unexpected triggers and navigate "the firsts" with compassion for myself. I commit to moving my body and embracing physical activity as a source of strength. I take decisive steps toward my goals, knowing that each action contributes to my growth and healing.

And we know that in *all* things God works for the good of those who love him, who have been called according to his purpose.

Romans 8:28 (NIV)

YOUR *Notes* :

STAY ORGANIZED.

17

Organization is key. Try your best to keep your space as organized as possible. An organized space will help you not feel overwhelmed and anxious; this includes your bedroom, bathroom, office space, car, etc. As a result, you'll have an inviting space and feel inspired to create and execute your tasks. Utilizing a planner, a calendar, or creating a to-do list can assist you with staying on track and not forgetting important tasks.

18

DON'T BE A SUPERHERO.

Don't try to be everything to everybody. Do what you can, if you can, but don't overextend yourself. You can't pour from an empty cup. Before you can help others with their needs, you have to help you help yourself first. You need Yourself! You needs You!

Self Care
ACTIVITIES

Choose any Self-Care Activity from the list below to complete today.

1. Read the Bible for 30 minutes ☐

2. Create a Vision Board ☐

3. Create a bedtime routine ☐

4. Go to bed 30 minutes early ☐

5. Spend time in nature or do an outside activity ☐

6. Make your favorite meal ☐

Be *sober*, be vigilant; because your adversary the devil, as a roaring lion, walketh about, seeking whom he may devour.

1 Peter 5:8 (KJV)

YOUR *Notes*:

19

GET THERAPY IF NEEDED.

If you need therapy, get it. Sometimes you may not have someone to talk to or you may not feel comfortable speaking to those around you. Therapy is a good outlet. It can help you process your feelings and emotions as you go through the grieving process, which can be an ongoing journey. In addition, see what benefits your employer offers; some employers offer therapy services for little to no cost.

20

PAY IT FORWARD.

Share the gift of sharing. If you encounter someone who is grieving, offer them compassion. If there's a tip that helped you along your grieving process, please share it with that person. Sometimes people feel like there is no hope for their situation but if they see that someone else made it through, then, they can make it through as well.

A TIME FOR GRATITUDE

What's a nice thing someone said to you or you said to someone else?
_____
_____
_____

Did anything surprise you today in a good way? Why did it feel special?
_____
_____
_____

Write about three things you're most grateful for this year.
_____
_____
_____

What's a tradition you enjoyed with your loved one?
_____
_____
_____

Don't worry about anything; instead, pray about *everything*...

Phillipians 4:6-7 (NLT)

YOUR *Notes*:

WATCH THE COMPANY YOU KEEP.

21

Be aware of the company you keep, the people who you surround yourself with. Whether good or bad, these people play a tremendous role in your healing journey. Ask God for discernment. Most of the time, those people who you least expect are wishing on your downfall or may even try to take advantage of you through this devastating time.

GIVE GRACE.

22

Everybody deals with death differently. If you haven't heard from a family member or friend in awhile since the passing of your loved one, don't be quick to anger by getting in your feelings, check up on them. Extend grace to them. The passing of your loved one impacted others as well. Other love ones, family members, and friends had a relationship with your loved one too and very well, may be having a hard time processing the loved one's death. If possible, share with them what you have been experiencing and what is helping you get through. The way in which you are handling the grieving process can give them some hope and help them with their grievances.

Daily Affirmations

Today, I stay organized and manage my tasks with intention, recognizing that I don't need to be a superhero. I seek therapy if needed, knowing it's a strength to ask for support. I commit to paying it forward and surrounding myself with positive, supportive people. I give grace to myself and others, understanding that kindness and understanding are essential on this journey.

This is my command-be strong and courageous! Do not be afraid or discouraged. For the Lord your God is with you *wherever* you go.

Joshua 1:9 (NLT)

YOUR *Notes*:

23. EXPECTATION.

Expect the great. Good things are coming your way. Everything is working out for your good. It may seem like your life is going through a storm right now, but this storm could be pushing you towards your purpose. Blessings on blessings will be birthed from this grief. For example, this book that you're reading was written within a year of my Mom's passing.

24. DON'T BE SCARED.

Don't be scared of anything. There's nothing to be scared of. Yes, this grieving process may seem scary, but just know that there's light at the end of the tunnel. God didn't give you the spirit of fear, but of power, love, and a sound mind. Walk into that scripture; believe the living word. Be bold. Be fearless and conquer this storm.

Self Care ACTIVITIES

Choose any Self-Care Activity from the list below to complete today.

1. Have a Spa Day ☐

2. Take a Nap ☐

3. Ask for help when you need it ☐

4. Buy something nice for yourself ☐

5. Share happiness with others ☐

6. Give to a Charity ☐

For God has not given us a spirit of fear and timidity, but of *power*, love, and a sound mind.

2 Timothy 1:7 (NLT)

YOUR *Notes* :

BE FEARLESS.

During this phase, it's important to be fearless. This may gradually take some time to achieve, but all of a sudden you'll get a boldness to live out your life. To take on life's challenges. You'll feel like, ""If I can survive making it through the passing of my loved one, I can do anything!"

25

26

ARMOR UP.

Pour into your spirit-man. Read the Bible. The Word will give you peace. Be intentional by setting the tone for your day. Keep positivity surrounded by you by listening and watching spiritual content. Spend time with the Lord. Praise! Worship! Pray!

GRATITUDE
WORD SEARCH

Find and circle all the words to be grateful for.

WARMTH	JOY	FREEDOM	PARTIES
PETS	LOVE	SCHOOL	FOOD
SEASONS	GAMES	FRIENDS	FAMILY

```
Q B F F R I E N D S
S W F Q S E A V S F
C A R P E D J P C A
E R E B A G N V H M
P M E F S R Z D O I
E T D O O O T U O L
T H O O N T N I L Y
S J M D S Y J L E X
G A M E S L O V E S
N V T S B P Y T Z W
```

Don't be afraid, for I am with you. Don't be discouraged, for I am your God. I will strengthen you and help you. I will hold you up with my *victorious* right hand.

Isaiah 41:10 (NLT)

YOUR *Notes*:

PRAY.

27

Pray without ceasing. Pray for family. Pray for friends. Pray for yourself. Cast your burdens to the Lord. When the weight of grief feels so heavy, give it to God. God will guide you through this process. He'll never leave you nor forsake you. He will be there for you always and forever. Put your trust in Him.

28

WATCH YOUR FOCUS.

Watch what you focus on. Try your best to avoid as many distractions as possible. What you focus on will grow, whether good or bad. If you focus on the bad, that's what you are putting out in the atmosphere and will receive. You'll notice that your stress level is increasing; aches and pains will be coming out of no where; however, if you focus on good things, you'll notice your stress level is less; you'll notice more peace and calmness within yourself.

Daily Affirmations

Today, I expect good things and embrace courage, choosing to be fearless in my journey. I arm myself with the Word of God, prayer, praise, and worship, trusting in God's protection and guidance. I remain mindful of my focus, joining a supportive community and allowing myself the time needed to grieve.

Good people pass away; the godly often pass away before their time. But no one seems to care or wonder why. No one seems to understand that God is *protecting* them from the evil to come.

Isaiah 57:1 (NLT)

YOUR *Notes* :

JOIN A COMMUNITY.

You are not alone. Many days you may feel like you are, but you are not.
Joining a community can assist you with becoming active and socializing with others. Join a community that suits your interests. This can include joining the gym near your neighborhood, a car club or even a thrifting community on social media just to name a few.

29

DON'T RUSH THE PROCESS.

Everyone's journey to healing is different. Some people may heal or be at peace with the passing of their loved one in a few months, a year, or more, but don't beat yourself up. You are stronger than you think, and you will get through this difficult time.

30

Self Care
ACTIVITIES

Choose any Self-Care Activity from the list below to complete today.

1. Watch a movie or TV show ☐

2. Check up on a family member ☐

3. Organize your Office ☐

4. Go to a Farmer's Market ☐

5. Listen to a motivational podcast ☐

6. Eat a healthy meal ☐

Consider it pure *joy* my brothers and sisters, whenever you face trials of any kind....

James 1:2 (NIV)

YOUR *Notes* :

YOUR *Notes*:

YOUR *Notes* :

YOUR *Notes*:

YOUR *Notes*:

YOUR *Notes* :

YOUR *Notes* :

YOUR *Notes*:

YOUR *Notes*:

YOUR *Notes*:

Conclusion

As we come to the end of "Journey of a Grieving Heart: 30 Devotions and Tips for Finding Peace and Embracing Life After the Loss of a Loved One," I encourage you to reflect on this path that we've traveled together. This book has shared practical and heartfelt tips that guided me through my personal journey of grief after the sudden loss of my mother. Each tip, whether it's letting God into your journey, practicing self-care, or setting boundaries, was a vital step toward adjusting to a new normal.

In conclusion, I revisit these essential insights and offer final reflections on finding hope amidst sorrow. Embracing the principles of gratitude, self-compassion, and community support can transform the journey through grief into a path of healing and renewal. As you continue forward, remember that while the pain of loss may never fully disappear, the strength and resilience you build can illuminate a path toward a meaningful and hopeful future.

May these tips serve as a guide and a source of comfort, reminding you that you are not alone and that every step taken in the direction of healing is a testament to your courage and capacity for renewal.

With Love,

Shannon J. Johnson

THE END

ACKNOWLEDGEMENTS

This body of work is dedicated to My Mommy.

Thank You to all of my family and friends for your love and support

❤️❤️❤️

thank you

Thank you for reading
"Journey of a Grieving Heart"!

Stay Connected

Thank you for being part of this journey. Together, we can make a difference!

If you found this book helpful, your feedback means the world to me! Please take a moment to leave a review on Amazon—your words can inspire others on their journey.

Feel free to share your thoughts on social media and tag me using the hashtag #JourneyOfAGrievingHeart. I'd love to connect with you!

Stay connected for exclusive content, new releases, and special offers by following me on the platforms below.

For more information:

@allthings_shannonjoy

allthings_shannonjoy

Linktree https://linktr.ee/shannonjoy

Made in the USA
Columbia, SC
03 December 2024